NOT YOUR TYPICAL BULLET JOURNAL

Writer/Illustrator: Shoshana Brand

Layout Design: Fetifolios

Not Your Typical Bujo

ISBN: 978-0-9978213-2-1

Layout Design: Fefifolios
Made in the USA, 2021

Own a Journal to Tell Your Tale

www.ajarbooks.com

When you bullet journal, you enter a sacred space within. You devote time and energy to your own soul.

You get away from interruptions and distractions to rejuvenate your inner being. You get connected with your creativity and your most individual concepts. You build awareness, and become calmer and more joyful.

Contemplate on the day before, and grow.
Plan your next day,
and you will see it manifested.

Have a blessed year.
Have a blessed life.

Love —

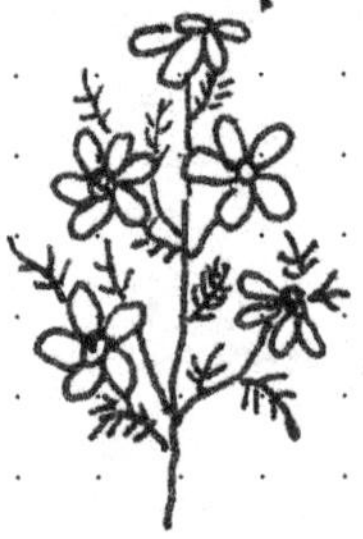

The creators of Ajar Books

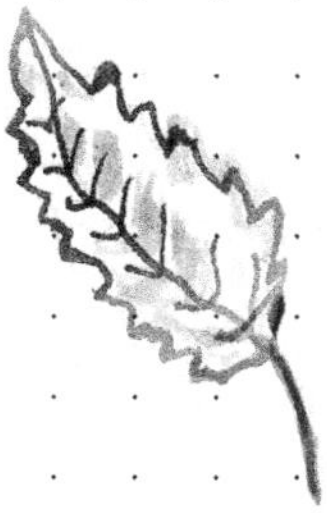

This Bujo Belongs to:

____

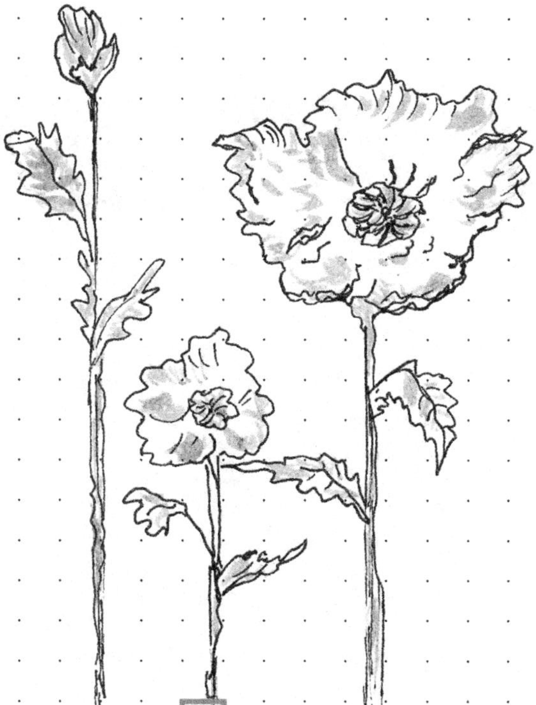

This is a bujo
WITH
SOME
hand-written
TABLES
AND GUIDELINES
to help you start journaling
EASILY.

You can follow it as is,
CHANGE it
or RECREATE it.

THIS IS **YOUR** BUJO.
Be light about it.

Enjoy.

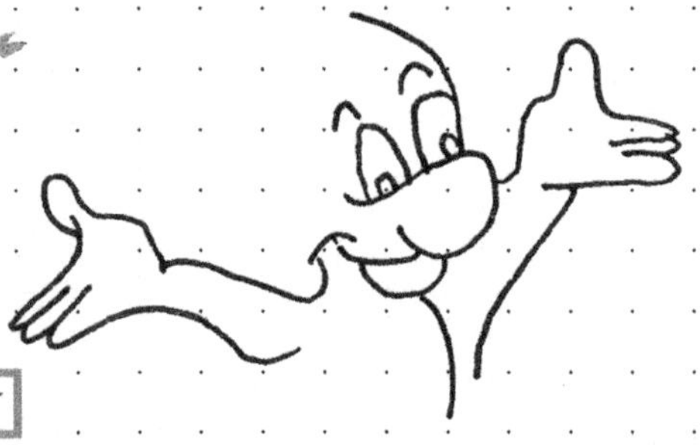

KEY:

∘ A TASK

× COMPLETED (an × over a dot)

> MIGRATED (moved to another day)

⊸ EVENT (such as a birthday)

~~CANCELED OR NOT RELEVANT~~ (crossing words)

✳ SOMETHING IMPORTANT

Many people also use different colored pencils, markers, and tapes in various colors.

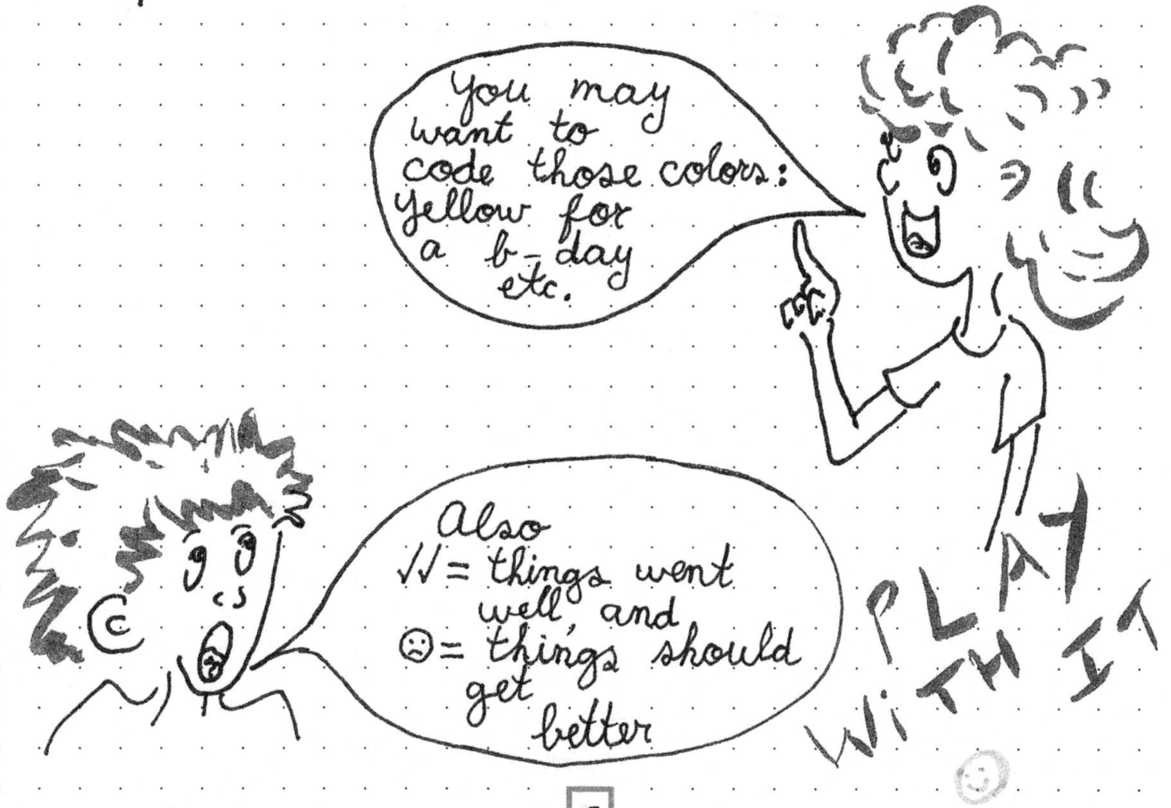

Tips For Journaling:

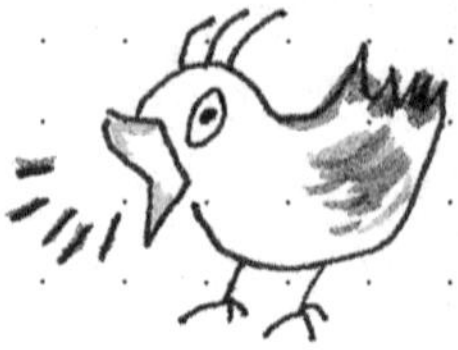

- Create a routine.
- Place this bujo close to you.
- Listen to your favorite music or eat a tasty snack when you journal.
- Not everything should be written down.
- Don't be hard on yourself.

My Insights on Journaling:

-

page #	CONTENT

page #	CONTENT

page #	CONTENT

page #	CONTENT
	Please start numbering your Bujo's pages

page #	CONTENT

page #	CONTENT

The tables for the 12 months of the year were drawn for you. Write down the name of each month.

Fill-in the dates of each month as each year is different.

A YEAR AT A GLANCE

JANUARY

M	T	W	T	F	S	S

DATES TO NOTE:

1
2
3
4
5
6
7
8
9
10
11
12
13
14
15
16
17
18
19
20
21
22
23
24
25
26
27
28
29
30
31

FEBRUARY

M	T	W	T	F	S	S

DATES TO NOTE:

1
2
3
4
5
6
7
8
9
10
11
12
13
14
15
16
17
18
19
20
21
22
23
24
25
26
27
28
29

MARCH

M	T	W	T	F	S	S

DATES TO NOTE:

1
2
3
4
5
6
7
8
9
10
11
12
13
14
15
16
17
18
19
20
21
22
23
24
25
26
27
28
29
30
31

A YEAR AT A GLANCE

APRIL

M	T	W	T	F	S	S

DATES TO NOTE:

1
2
3
4
5
6
7
8
9
10
11
12
13
14
15
16
17
18
19
20
21
22
23
24
25
26
27
28
29
30

MAY

M	T	W	T	F	S	S

DATES TO NOTE:

1
2
3
4
5
6
7
8
9
10
11
12
13
14
15
16
17
18
19
20
21
22
23
24
25
26
27
28
29
30
31

JUNE

M	T	W	T	F	S	S

DATES TO NOTE:

1
2
3
4
5
6
7
8
9
10
11
12
13
14
15
16
17
18
19
20
21
22
23
24
25
26
27
28
29
30

A YEAR AT A GLANCE

JULY

M	T	W	T	F	S	S

DATES TO NOTE:

1
2
3
4
5
6
7
8
9
10
11
12
13
14
15
16
17
18
19
20
21
22
23
24
25
26
27
28
29
30
31

AUGUST

M	T	W	T	F	S	S

DATES TO NOTE:

1
2
3
4
5
6
7
8
9
10
11
12
13
14
15
16
17
18
19
20
21
22
23
24
25
26
27
28
29
30
31

SEPTEMBER

M	T	W	T	F	S	S

DATES TO NOTE:

1
2
3
4
5
6
7
8
9
10
11
12
13
14
15
16
17
18
19
20
21
22
23
24
25
26
27
28
29
30

A YEAR AT A GLANCE

OCTOBER

M	T	W	T	F	S	S

DATES TO NOTE:

1
2
3
4
5
6
7
8
9
10
11
12
13
14
15
16
17
18
19
20
21
22
23
24
25
26
27
28
29
30
31

NOVEMBER

M	T	W	T	F	S	S

DATES TO NOTE:

1
2
3
4
5
6
7
8
9
10
11
12
13
14
15
16
17
18
19
20
21
22
23
24
25
26
27
28
29
30

DECEMBER

M	T	W	T	F	S	S

DATES TO NOTE:

1
2
3
4
5
6
7
8
9
10
11
12
13
14
15
16
17
18
19
20
21
22
23
24
25
26
27
28
29
30
31

You are covered here
for any year
that you wish
to create
a bujo. (Even a leap year such as 2022)

WRITE DOWN THE NAMES OF THE MONTHS

AND

TRANSFER RELEVANT DATES

FROM

"THE YEAR AT A GLANCE"

TO THE FOLLOWING PAGES

A MONTH AT A GLANCE

M	T	W	T	F	S	S

my monthly mantra:

CHECK-IN

How I Feel:

Physically

Emotionally

Spiritually

Relationships

BRAIN DUMP

Ideas

Wishes

Resolutions

Accomplishments

HABIT TRACKER SAMPLE AND GUIDELINES

FITNESS

M	T	W	Th	F	S	S
						1
2	3	4	5	6	7	8
9	10	11	12	13	14	15
16	17	18	19	20	21	22
23	24	25	26	27	28	29
30	31	SAMPLE				

DIET

M	T	W	Th	F	S	S

SPIRITUALITY

M	T	W	Th	F	S	S

BOOK CLUB

M	T	W	Th	F	S	S

This tracker is here to build awareness, not to create guilt. Be light about it.

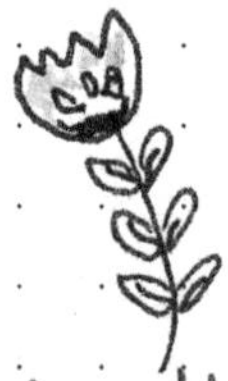

Create your own "Habit Tracker" in the following page and in the future months.

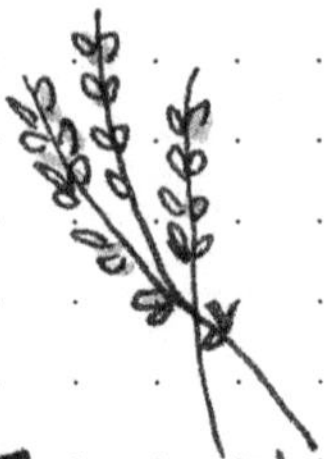

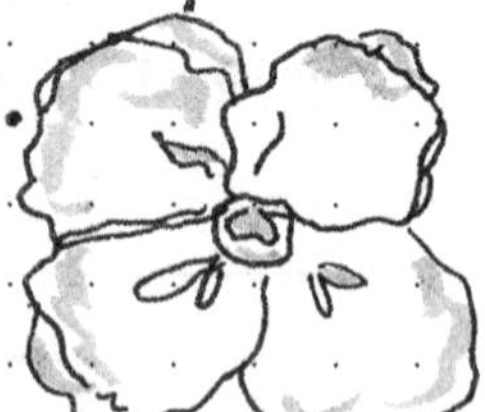

In each chart we drew enough rectangles for any month in any year. Write a date in each blank space to match the day.

HABIT TRACKER

M	T	W	Th	F	S	S

M	T	W	Th	F	S	S

M	T	W	Th	F	S	S

M	T	W	Th	F	S	S

M	T	W	Th	F	S	S

M	T	W	Th	F	S	S

M	T	W	Th	F	S	S

M	T	W	Th	F	S	S

GRATITUDES:

1.
2.
3.

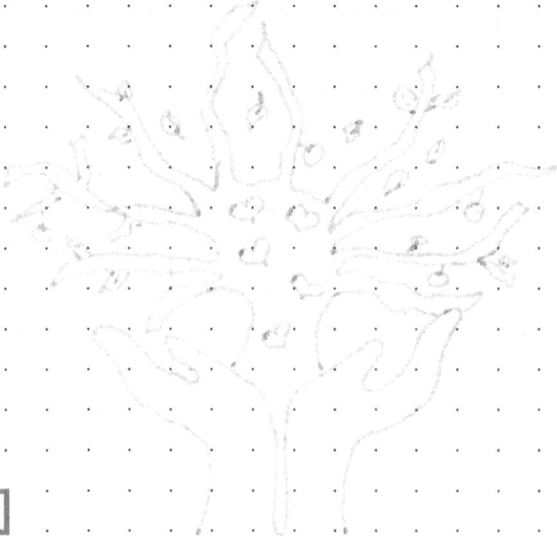

NOTES and DOODLES

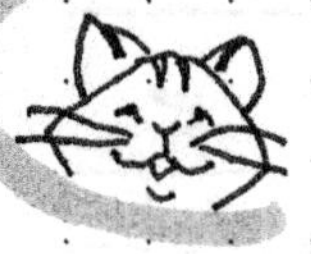

A MONTH AT A GLANCE

M	T	W	T	F	S	S

my monthly mantra:

CHECK-IN

How I Feel:

Physically

Emotionally

Spiritually

Relationships

BRAIN DUMP

Ideas

Wishes

Resolutions

Accomplishments

HABIT TRACKER

M	T	W	Th	F	S	S

M	T	W	Th	F	S	S

M	T	W	Th	F	S	S

M	T	W	Th	F	S	S

M	T	W	Th	F	S	S

M	T	W	Th	F	S	S

M	T	W	Th	F	S	S

M	T	W	Th	F	S	S

GRATITUDES:

1.
2.
3.

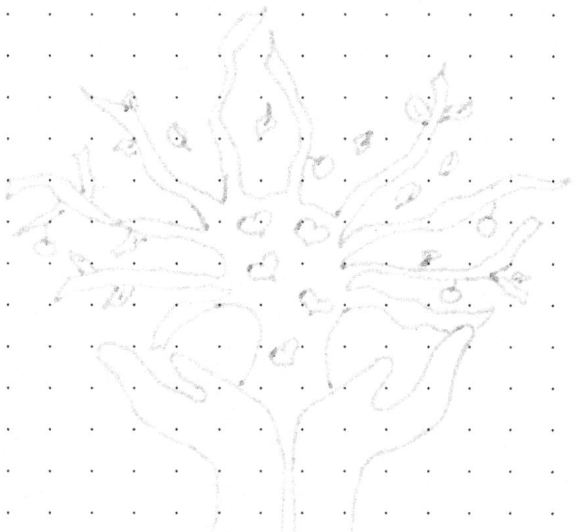

NOTES and DOODLES

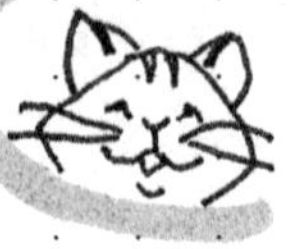

A MONTH AT A GLANCE

M	T	W	T	F	S	S

my monthly mantra:

CHECK-IN

How I Feel:

Physically

Emotionally

Spiritually

Relationships

BRAIN DUMP

Ideas

Wishes

Resolutions

Accomplishments

HABIT TRACKER

M	T	W	Th	F	S	S

M	T	W	Th	F	S	S

M	T	W	Th	F	S	S

M	T	W	Th	F	S	S

M	T	W	Th	F	S	S

M	T	W	Th	F	S	S

M	T	W	Th	F	S	S

M	T	W	Th	F	S	S

GRATITUDES:

1.
2.
3.

NOTES and DOODLES

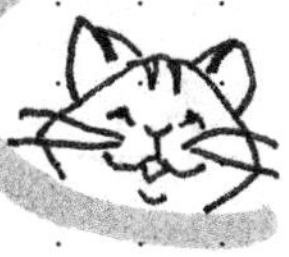

A MONTH AT A GLANCE

M	T	W	T	F	S	S

my monthly mantra:

CHECK-IN

How I Feel:

Physically

Emotionally

Spiritually

Relationships

BRAIN DUMP

Ideas

Wishes

Resolutions

Accomplishments

HABIT TRACKER

M	T	W	Th	F	S	S

M	T	W	Th	F	S	S

M	T	W	Th	F	S	S

M	T	W	Th	F	S	S

M	T	W	Th	F	S	S

M	T	W	Th	F	S	S

M	T	W	Th	F	S	S

M	T	W	Th	F	S	S

GRATITUDES:

1.
2.
3.

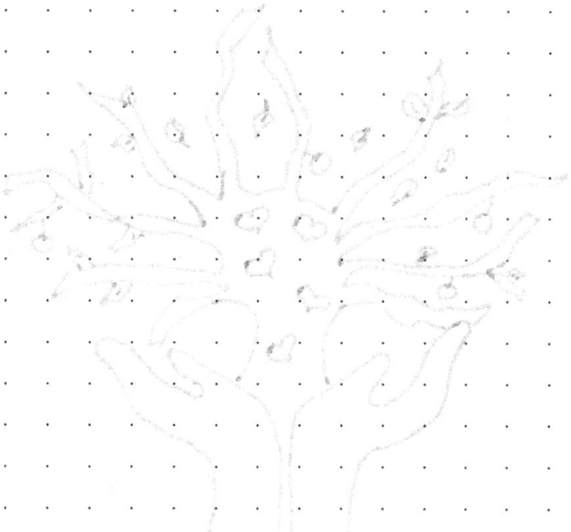

NOTES and DOODLES

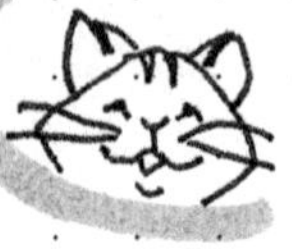

A MONTH AT A GLANCE

M	T	W	T	F	S	S

my monthly mantra:

CHECK-IN

How I Feel:

Physically

Emotionally

Spiritually

Relationships

BRAIN DUMP

Ideas

Wishes

Resolutions

Accomplishments

HABIT TRACKER

M	T	W	Th	F	S	S

M	T	W	Th	F	S	S

M	T	W	Th	F	S	S

M	T	W	Th	F	S	S

M	T	W	Th	F	S	S

M	T	W	Th	F	S	S

M	T	W	Th	F	S	S

M	T	W	Th	F	S	S

GRATITUDES:

1.
2.
3.

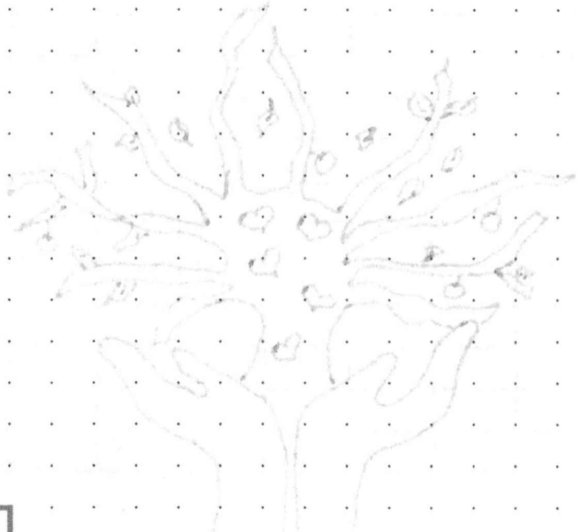

NOTES and DOODLES

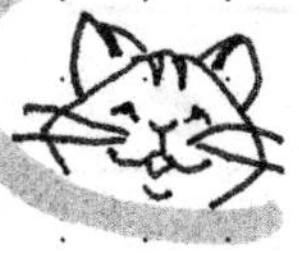

A MONTH AT A GLANCE

M	T	W	T	F	S	S

my monthly mantra:

CHECK-IN

How I Feel:

Physically

Emotionally

Spiritually

Relationships

BRAIN DUMP

Ideas

Wishes

Resolutions

Accomplishments

HABIT TRACKER

M	T	W	Th	F	S	S

M	T	W	Th	F	S	S

M	T	W	Th	F	S	S

M	T	W	Th	F	S	S

M	T	W	Th	F	S	S

M	T	W	Th	F	S	S

M	T	W	Th	F	S	S

M	T	W	Th	F	S	S

GRATITUDES:

1.
2.
3.

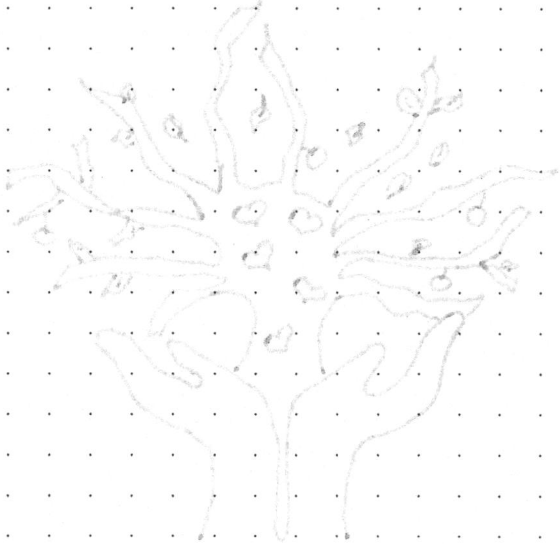

NOTES and DOODLES

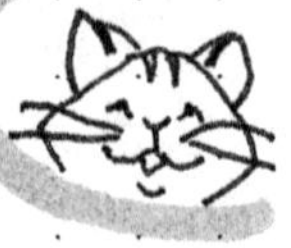

A MONTH AT A GLANCE

M	T	W	T	F	S	S

my monthly mantra:

CHECK-IN

How I Feel:

Physically

Emotionally

Spiritually

Relationships

BRAIN DUMP

Ideas

Wishes

Resolutions

Accomplishments

HABIT TRACKER

M	T	W	Th	F	S	S

M	T	W	Th	F	S	S

M	T	W	Th	F	S	S

M	T	W	Th	F	S	S

M	T	W	Th	F	S	S

M	T	W	Th	F	S	S

M	T	W	Th	F	S	S

M	T	W	Th	F	S	S

GRATITUDES:

1.
2.
3.

NOTES and DOODLES

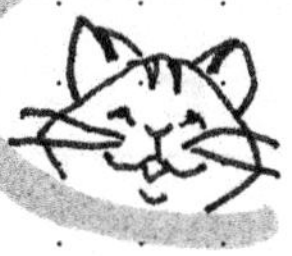

A MONTH AT A GLANCE

M	T	W	T	F	S	S

my monthly mantra:

CHECK-IN

How I Feel:

Physically

Emotionally

Spiritually

Relationships

BRAIN DUMP

Ideas

Wishes

Resolutions

Accomplishments

HABIT TRACKER

M	T	W	Th	F	S	S

M	T	W	Th	F	S	S

M	T	W	Th	F	S	S

M	T	W	Th	F	S	S

M	T	W	Th	F	S	S

M	T	W	Th	F	S	S

M	T	W	Th	F	S	S

M	T	W	Th	F	S	S

GRATITUDES:

1.
2.
3.

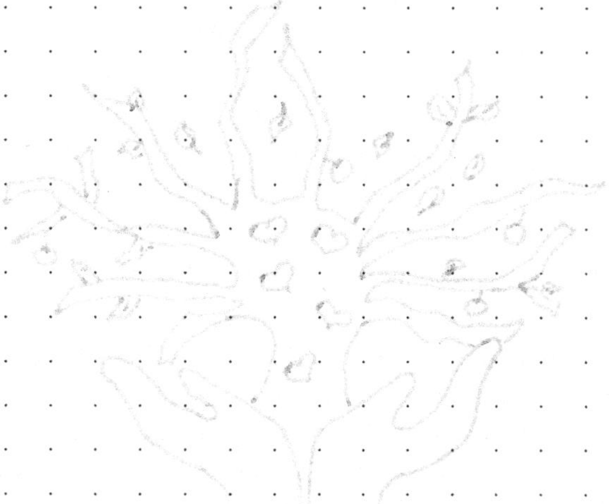

NOTES and DOODLES

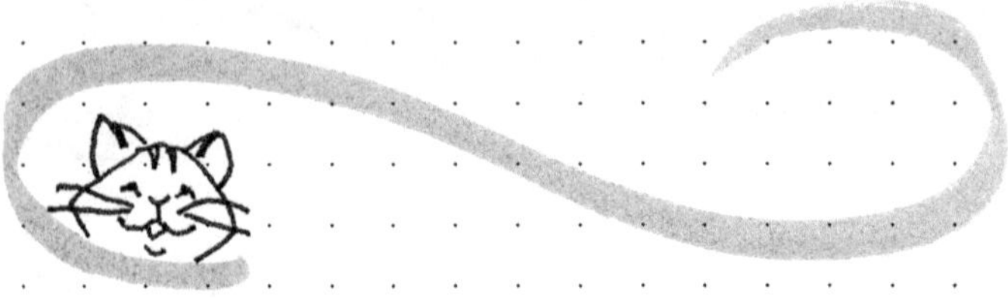

A MONTH AT A GLANCE

M	T	W	T	F	S	S

my monthly mantra:

CHECK-IN

How I Feel:

Physically

Emotionally

Spiritually

Relationships

BRAIN DUMP

Ideas

Wishes

Resolutions

Accomplishments

HABIT TRACKER

M	T	W	Th	F	S	S

M	T	W	Th	F	S	S

M	T	W	Th	F	S	S

M	T	W	Th	F	S	S

M	T	W	Th	F	S	S

M	T	W	Th	F	S	S

M	T	W	Th	F	S	S

M	T	W	Th	F	S	S

GRATITUDES:

1.
2.
3.

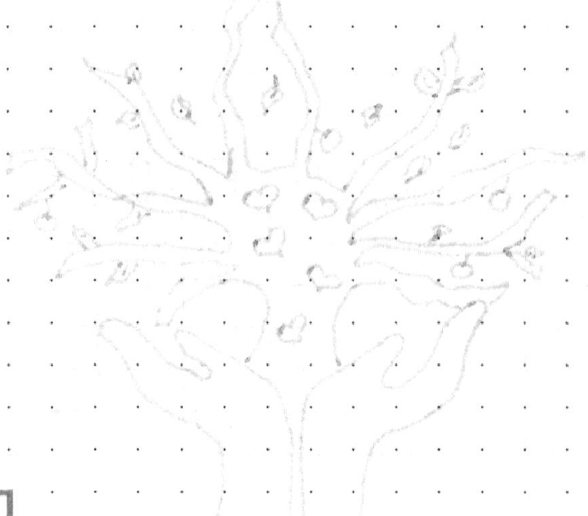

NOTES and DOODLES

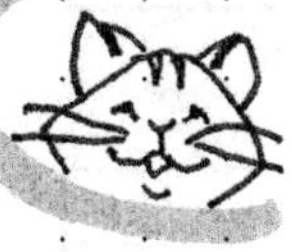

A MONTH AT A GLANCE

M	T	W	T	F	S	S

my monthly mantra:

CHECK-IN

How I Feel:

Physically

Emotionally

Spiritually

Relationships

BRAIN DUMP

Ideas

Wishes

Resolutions

Accomplishments

HABIT TRACKER

M	T	W	Th	F	S	S

M	T	W	Th	F	S	S

M	T	W	Th	F	S	S

M	T	W	Th	F	S	S

M	T	W	Th	F	S	S

M	T	W	Th	F	S	S

M	T	W	Th	F	S	S

M	T	W	Th	F	S	S

GRATITUDES:

1.
2.
3.

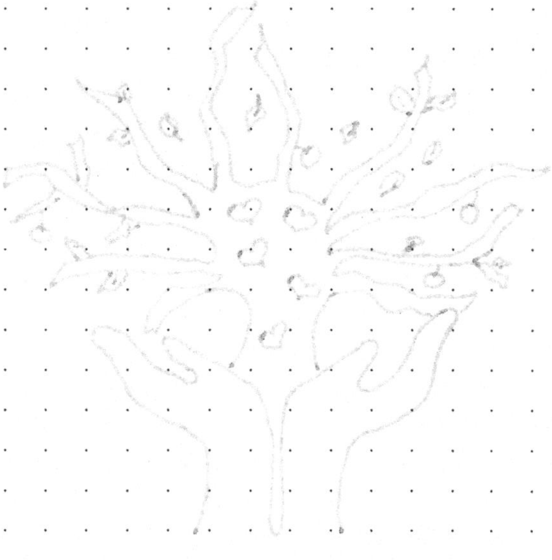

NOTES and DOODLES

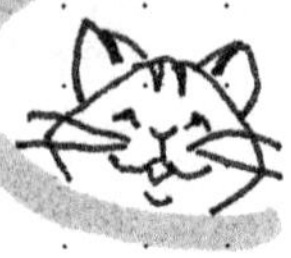

A MONTH AT A GLANCE

M T W T F S S

my monthly mantra:

CHECK-IN

How I Feel:

Physically

Emotionally

Spiritually

Relationships

BRAIN DUMP

Ideas

Wishes

Resolutions

Accomplishments

HABIT TRACKER

M	T	W	Th	F	S	S

M	T	W	Th	F	S	S

M	T	W	Th	F	S	S

M	T	W	Th	F	S	S

M	T	W	Th	F	S	S

M	T	W	Th	F	S	S

M	T	W	Th	F	S	S

M	T	W	Th	F	S	S

GRATITUDES:

1.
2.
3.

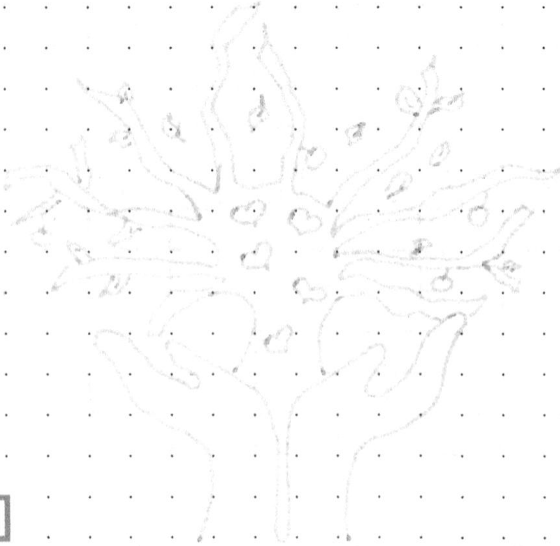

NOTES and DOODLES

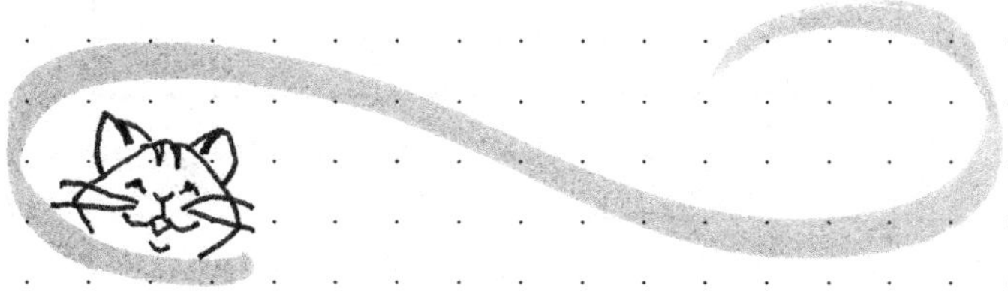

A MONTH AT A GLANCE

M	T	W	T	F	S	S

my monthly mantra:

CHECK-IN

How I Feel:

Physically

Emotionally

Spiritually

Relationships

BRAIN DUMP

Ideas

Wishes

Resolutions

Accomplishments

HABIT TRACKER

M	T	W	Th	F	S	S

M	T	W	Th	F	S	S

M	T	W	Th	F	S	S

M	T	W	Th	F	S	S

M	T	W	Th	F	S	S

M	T	W	Th	F	S	S

M	T	W	Th	F	S	S

M	T	W	Th	F	S	S

GRATITUDES:

1.
2.
3.

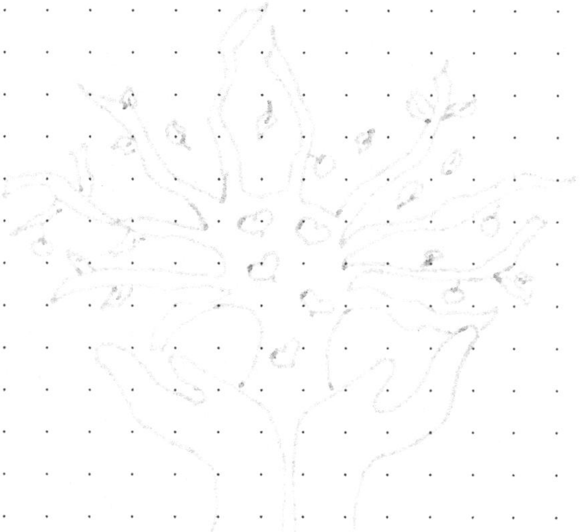

NOTES and DOODLES

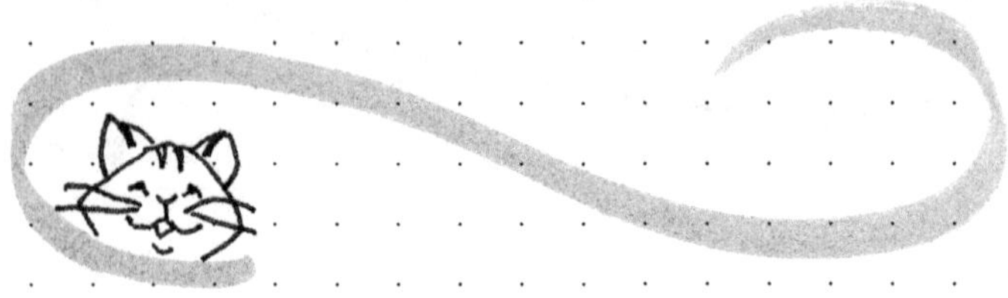

A WEEK AT A GLANCE

	Mon.	Tues.	Wed.	Thur.	Fri	Sat.
Morning						
After noon						
Evening						

NOTES:	SUNDAY

A WEEK AT A GLANCE

	Mon.	Tues.	Wed.	Thur.	Fri	Sat.
Morning						
After noon						
Evening						

NOTES:	SUNDAY

A WEEK AT A GLANCE

	Mon.	Tues.	Wed.	Thur.	Fri	Sat.
Morning						
After noon						
Evening						

NOTES:	SUNDAY

A WEEK AT A GLANCE

	Mon.	Tues.	Wed.	Thur.	Fri	Sat.
Morning						
Afternoon						
Evening						

NOTES:

SUNDAY

A WEEK AT A GLANCE

	Mon.	Tues.	Wed.	Thur.	Fri	Sat.
Morning						
After noon						
Evening						

NOTES:	SUNDAY

A WEEK AT A GLANCE

	Mon.	Tues.	Wed.	Thur.	Fri	Sat.
Morning						
After noon						
Evening						

NOTES:	SUNDAY

A WEEK AT A GLANCE

	Mon.	Tues.	Wed.	Thur.	Fri	Sat.
Morning						
After noon						
Evening						

NOTES:	SUNDAY

A WEEK AT A GLANCE

	Mon.	Tues.	Wed.	Thur.	Fri	Sat.
Morning						
After noon						
Evening						

NOTES:	SUNDAY

A WEEK AT A GLANCE

	Mon.	Tues.	Wed.	Thur.	Fri	Sat.
Morning						
After noon						
Evening						

NOTES:	SUNDAY

A WEEK AT A GLANCE

	Mon.	Tues.	Wed.	Thur.	Fri	Sat.
Morning						
After noon						
Evening						

NOTES:	SUNDAY

A WEEK AT A GLANCE

	Mon.	Tues.	Wed.	Thur.	Fri	Sat.
Morning						
After noon						
Evening						

NOTES:

SUNDAY

A WEEK AT A GLANCE

	Mon.	Tues.	Wed.	Thur.	Fri	Sat.
Morning						
Afternoon						
Evening						

NOTES:	SUNDAY

A WEEK AT A GLANCE

	Mon.	Tues.	Wed.	Thur.	Fri	Sat.
Morning						
After noon						
Evening						

NOTES:

SUNDAY

A WEEK AT A GLANCE

	Mon.	Tues.	Wed.	Thur.	Fri	Sat.
Morning						
After noon						
Evening						

NOTES:	SUNDAY

A WEEK AT A GLANCE

	Mon.	Tues.	Wed.	Thur.	Fri	Sat.
Morning						
After noon						
Evening						

NOTES:

SUNDAY

A WEEK AT A GLANCE

☀ ☾	Mon.	Tues.	Wed.	Thur.	Fri	Sat.
Morning						
After noon						
Evening						

NOTES:	SUNDAY

A WEEK AT A GLANCE

	Mon.	Tues.	Wed.	Thur.	Fri	Sat.
Morning						
After noon						
Evening						

NOTES:	SUNDAY

A WEEK AT A GLANCE

	Mon.	Tues.	Wed.	Thur.	Fri	Sat.
Morning						
After noon						
Evening						

NOTES:

SUNDAY

A WEEK AT A GLANCE

	Mon.	Tues.	Wed.	Thur.	Fri	Sat.
Morning						
Afternoon						
Evening						

NOTES:	SUNDAY

A WEEK AT A GLANCE

	Mon.	Tues.	Wed.	Thur.	Fri	Sat.
Morning						
After noon						
Evening						

NOTES:	SUNDAY

A WEEK AT A GLANCE

	Mon.	Tues.	Wed.	Thur.	Fri	Sat.
Morning						
After noon						
Evening						

NOTES:	SUNDAY

A WEEK AT A GLANCE

	Mon.	Tues.	Wed.	Thur.	Fri	Sat.
Morning						
After noon						
Evening						

NOTES:	SUNDAY

A WEEK AT A GLANCE

	Mon.	Tues.	Wed.	Thur.	Fri	Sat.
Morning						
After noon						
Evening						

NOTES:

SUNDAY

A WEEK AT A GLANCE

	Mon.	Tues.	Wed.	Thur.	Fri	Sat.
Morning						
After noon						
Evening						

NOTES:

SUNDAY

A WEEK AT A GLANCE

	Mon.	Tues.	Wed.	Thur.	Fri	Sat.
Morning						
Afternoon						
Evening						

NOTES:	SUNDAY

A WEEK AT A GLANCE

	Mon.	Tues.	Wed.	Thur.	Fri	Sat.
Morning						
After noon						
Evening						

NOTES:	SUNDAY

A WEEK AT A GLANCE

	Mon.	Tues.	Wed.	Thur.	Fri	Sat.
Morning						
After noon						
Evening						

NOTES:

SUNDAY

A WEEK AT A GLANCE

☼ ☾	Mon.	Tues.	Wed.	Thur.	Fri	Sat.
Morning						
After noon						
Evening						

NOTES:	SUNDAY

A WEEK AT A GLANCE

	Mon.	Tues.	Wed.	Thur.	Fri	Sat.
Morning						
After noon						
Evening						

NOTES:	SUNDAY

A WEEK AT A GLANCE

	Mon.	Tues.	Wed.	Thur.	Fri	Sat.
Morning						
After noon						
Evening						

NOTES:

SUNDAY

A WEEK AT A GLANCE

	Mon.	Tues.	Wed.	Thur.	Fri	Sat.
Morning						
Afternoon						
Evening						

NOTES:	SUNDAY

A WEEK AT A GLANCE

	Mon.	Tues.	Wed.	Thur.	Fri	Sat.
Morning						
After noon						
Evening						

NOTES:	SUNDAY

A WEEK AT A GLANCE

	Mon.	Tues.	Wed.	Thur.	Fri	Sat.
Morning						
After noon						
Evening						

NOTES:	SUNDAY

A WEEK AT A GLANCE

	Mon.	Tues.	Wed.	Thur.	Fri	Sat.
Morning						
After noon						
Evening						

NOTES:	SUNDAY

A WEEK AT A GLANCE

	Mon.	Tues.	Wed.	Thur.	Fri	Sat.
Morning						
After noon						
Evening						

NOTES:

SUNDAY

A WEEK AT A GLANCE

	Mon.	Tues.	Wed.	Thur.	Fri	Sat.
Morning						
After noon						
Evening						

NOTES:	SUNDAY

A WEEK AT A GLANCE

	Mon.	Tues.	Wed.	Thur.	Fri	Sat.
Morning						
After noon						
Evening						

NOTES:	SUNDAY

A WEEK AT A GLANCE

	Mon.	Tues.	Wed.	Thur.	Fri	Sat.
Morning						
After noon						
Evening						

NOTES:	SUNDAY

A WEEK AT A GLANCE

	Mon.	Tues.	Wed.	Thur.	Fri	Sat.
Morning						
After noon						
Evening						

NOTES:	SUNDAY

A WEEK AT A GLANCE

	Mon.	Tues.	Wed.	Thur.	Fri	Sat.
Morning						
After noon						
Evening						

NOTES:	SUNDAY

A WEEK AT A GLANCE

	Mon.	Tues.	Wed.	Thur.	Fri	Sat.
Morning						
After noon						
Evening						

NOTES:	SUNDAY

A WEEK AT A GLANCE

	Mon.	Tues.	Wed.	Thur.	Fri	Sat.
Morning						
After noon						
Evening						

NOTES:	SUNDAY

A WEEK AT A GLANCE

☼ ☾	Mon.	Tues.	Wed.	Thur.	Fri	Sat.
Morning						
After noon						
Evening						

NOTES:	SUNDAY

A WEEK AT A GLANCE

	Mon.	Tues.	Wed.	Thur.	Fri	Sat.
Morning						
After noon						
Evening						

NOTES:

SUNDAY

A WEEK AT A GLANCE

	Mon.	Tues.	Wed.	Thur.	Fri	Sat.
Morning						
After noon						
Evening						

NOTES:	SUNDAY

A WEEK AT A GLANCE

	Mon.	Tues.	Wed.	Thur.	Fri	Sat.
Morning						
After noon						
Evening						

NOTES:	SUNDAY

A WEEK AT A GLANCE

☼ ☾	Mon.	Tues.	Wed.	Thur.	Fri	Sat.
Morning						
After noon						
Evening						

NOTES:	SUNDAY

A WEEK AT A GLANCE

	Mon.	Tues.	Wed.	Thur.	Fri	Sat.
Morning						
After noon						
Evening						

NOTES:

SUNDAY

A WEEK AT A GLANCE

	Mon.	Tues.	Wed.	Thur.	Fri	Sat.
Morning						
Afternoon						
Evening						

NOTES:	SUNDAY

A WEEK AT A GLANCE

	Mon.	Tues.	Wed.	Thur.	Fri	Sat.
Morning						
Afternoon						
Evening						

NOTES:	SUNDAY

A WEEK AT A GLANCE

	Mon.	Tues.	Wed.	Thur.	Fri	Sat.
Morning						
After noon						
Evening						

NOTES:	SUNDAY

A WEEK AT A GLANCE

	Mon.	Tues.	Wed.	Thur.	Fri	Sat.
Morning						
After noon						
Evening						

NOTES:	SUNDAY

A WEEK AT A GLANCE

	Mon.	Tues.	Wed.	Thur.	Fri	Sat.
Morning						
After noon						
Evening						

NOTES:	SUNDAY

A WEEK AT A GLANCE

	Mon.	Tues.	Wed.	Thur.	Fri	Sat.
Morning						
After noon						
Evening						

NOTES:	SUNDAY

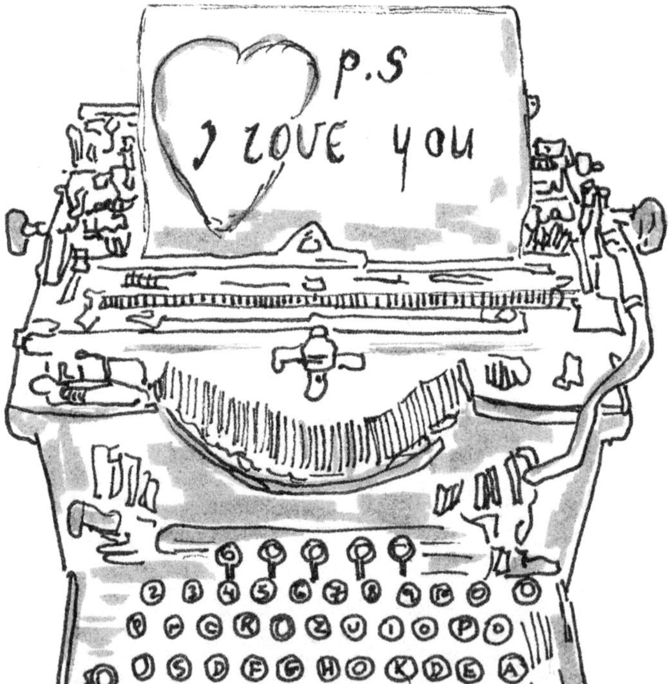
P.S
I LOVE you

Made in CA and TX, USA, 2021

Made in the USA
Monee, IL
08 November 2026

67971456R00116